the world's a dad

the world's a

Eric Grimes

dad

STERLING/HOLLAN
An imprint of Sterling Publishing Co., Inc.

New York / London
www.sterlingpublishing.com

In the eyes of their young children, every dad is an A-list celebrity. When we are small, we idolize him, marveling at the size of his enormous shoes, the strength of his arms when he swoops us into the air, and the way he can turn anything—even making a sandwich or taking a bath—into a fun and exciting adventure. We grow up thinking that our dads are fearless and indestructible. When we are old enough to know that they are human like everyone else, we love them even more deeply.

The world is blessed with devoted dads who show their kids how to live life to its fullest. If you think back, you'll probably remember that it was your father who taught you how to swim, ride a bike, drive, play ball, or dance around like a monkey!

This book is a photographic tribute to dads everywhere—from all corners of the globe and every creature of the animal kingdom. What better way to thank him for all those valuable lessons he taught you, how safe he made you feel as a kid, and how wonderful your life is because he's in it.

What a dreadful thing it must be
to have a dull father.

Mary Mapes Dodge

A truly rich man is one
whose children run into his arms
when his hands are empty.

Anonymous

One father is enough to govern one hundred sons, but not a hundred sons one father.

George Herbert

It is a wise father that knows his own child.

William Shakespeare

The father of a daughter is nothing but a high-class hostage. A father turns a stony face to his sons, berates them, shakes his antlers, paws the ground, snorts, runs them off into the under-brush, but when his daughter puts her arm over his shoulder and says, "Daddy, I need to ask you something," he is a pat of butter in a hot frying pan.

Garrison Keillor

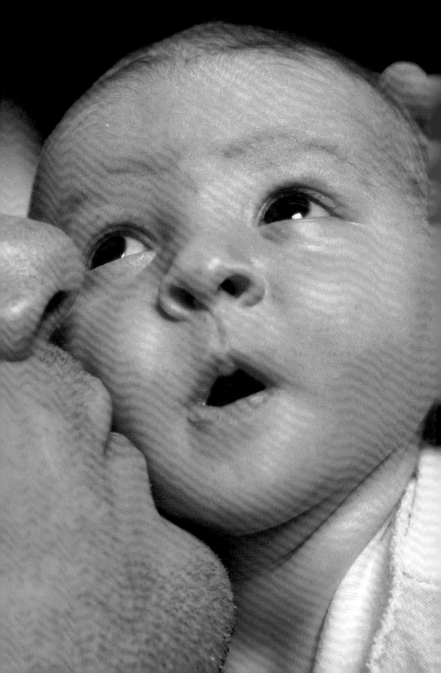

Fathers, like mothers, are not born.
Men grow into fathers and fathering is a
very important stage in their development.

David M. Gottesman

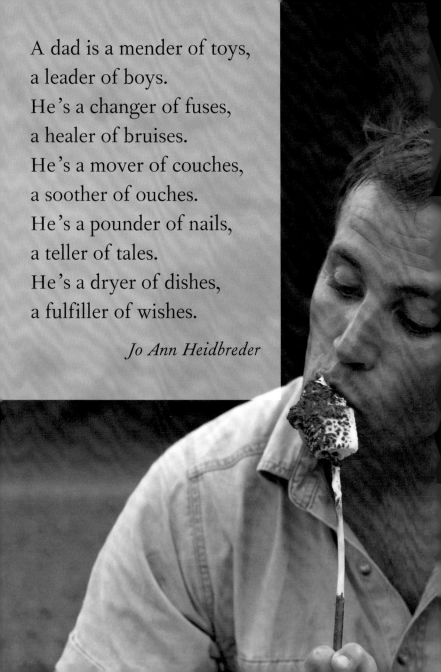

A dad is a mender of toys,
a leader of boys.
He's a changer of fuses,
a healer of bruises.
He's a mover of couches,
a soother of ouches.
He's a pounder of nails,
a teller of tales.
He's a dryer of dishes,
a fulfiller of wishes.

Jo Ann Heidbreder

I cannot think of any need in childhood as strong as the need for a father's protection.

Sigmund Freud

My father didn't tell me how to live;
he lived, and let me watch him do it.

Clarence B. Kelland

Blessed indeed is the man who hears many gentle voices call him father!

Lydia M. Child

A good father is one of the most unsung, unpraised, unnoticed, and yet one of the most valuable assets in our society.

Billy Graham

The good father does not have to be perfect. Rather, he has to be good enough to help his daughter to become a woman who is reasonably self-confident, self-sufficient, and free of crippling self-doubt, and to feel at ease "in the company of men."

Victoria Secunda

The most effective guard against delinquency is a father who is at the same time both strict and loving.

Sheldon Glueck

To her the name of father
was another name for love.

Fanny Fern

It doesn't matter who my father was;
it matters who I remember he was.

Anne Sexton

A father is a fellow who has replaced the currency in his wallet with the snapshots of his kids.

Anonymous

By the time a man realizes that maybe his father was right, he usually has a son who thinks he's wrong.

Charles Wadsworth

A father is always making his baby into a little woman. And when she is a woman he turns her back again.

Enid Bagnold

When a father gives to his son,
both laugh; when a son gives
to his father, both cry.

Jewish Proverb

He who is taught to live upon little owes more to his father's wisdom than he who has a great deal left him does to his father's care.

William Penn

Fatherhood is pretending the present you love most is soap-on-a-rope.

Bill Cosby

A man knows when he is growing old because he begins to look like his father.

Gabriel García Márquez

It's very important to lose graciously.
My dad taught me that.

Jack Nicklaus

Dad needs to show an incredible amount of respect and humor and friendship toward his mate so the kids understand their parents are sexy, they're fun, they do things together, they're best friends. Kids learn by example. If I respect Mom, they're going to respect Mom.

Tim Allen

An effective father devotes himself
to become an instrument and model of
human experience to his children . . .
accepts and affirms his children
for who they are, appreciates them
for what they are accomplishing,
and covers them with affection
because they are his.

Gordon MacDonald

A wise son maketh a glad father.

Proverbs 10:1

Like father, like son.

Chinese Proverb

You don't need to be right all the time. Your child wants a man for a father, not a formula. He wants real parents, real people capable of making mistakes without moping about it.

C. D. Williams

One night a father overheard
his son pray: "Dear God,
Make me the kind of man my daddy is."
Later that night, the father prayed,
"Dear God, Make me the kind of man
my son wants me to be."

Anonymous

It is not flesh and blood but the heart which makes us fathers and sons.

Johann Schiller

The father who loves his children will not substitute toys for time, replace commendation with condemnation, but will be their teacher not taskmaster.

Robert Flatt

Be kind to thy father,
for when thou were young,
who loved thee so fondly as he?
He caught the first accents
that fell from thy tongue,
and joined in thy innocent glee.

Margaret Courtney

It is admirable for a man to take his son fishing, but there is a special place in heaven for the father who takes his daughter shopping.

John Sinor

When I was a boy of fourteen,
my father was so ignorant I could
hardly stand to have the old man
around. But when I got to be
twenty-one, I was astonished at
how much he had learned in
seven years.

Mark Twain

Noble fathers have noble children.

Euripides

A new father quickly learns that his child invariably comes to the bathroom at precisely the times when he's in there, as if he needed company. The only way for this father to be certain of bathroom privacy is to shave at the gas station.

Bill Cosby

To a father growing old, nothing is dearer than a daughter.

Euripides

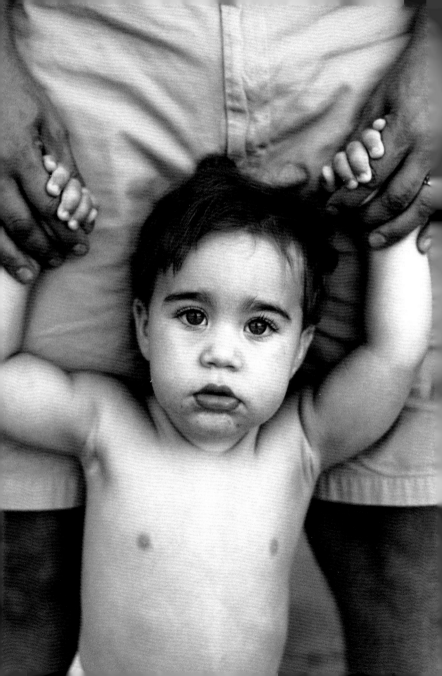

Everything I ever learned as a small boy came from my father. And I never found anything he ever told me to be wrong or worthless. The simple lessons he taught me are as sharp and clear in my mind, as if I had heard them only yesterday.

Philip Dunne

When you teach your son,
you teach your son's son.

The Talmud

A man's desire for a son is usually nothing but the wish to duplicate himself in order that such a remarkable pattern may not be lost to the world.

Helen Rowland

Until you have a son of your own . . .
you will never know the joy, the
love beyond feeling that resonates
in the heart of a father as he looks
upon his son.

Kent Nerburn

My dad has always taught me these words: care and share. The only thing I can do is try to give back.

Tiger Woods

My father once said,
"If the whole world wants to go left and you feel like going right, go right. You don't have to follow. You don't have to make a big deal about which way you're going. Just go. It's very easy."

Yanni

All the feeling which my father
could not put into words was
in his hand—any dog, child,
or horse would recognize the
kindness of it.

Freya Stark

You know, fathers just have a way
of putting everything together.

Erika Cosby

STERLING and the distinctive Sterling logo are registered
trademarks of Sterling Publishing Co., Inc.

Library of Congress Cataloging-in-Publication Data Available
10 9 8 7 6 5 4 3 2 1

Produced by Hollan Publishing, Inc.
100 Cummings Center, Suite 125G
Beverly, MA 01915
© 2008 by Hollan Publishing, Inc.

Published by Sterling Publishing Co., Inc.
387 Park Avenue South, New York, NY 10016

Distributed in Canada by Sterling Publishing
c/o Canadian Manda Group, 165 Dufferin Street
Toronto, Ontario, Canada M6K 3H6
Distributed in the United Kingdom
by GMC Distribution Services
Castle Place, 166 High Street, Lewes, East Sussex,
England BN7 1XU
Distributed in Australia by Capricorn Link (Australia) Pty. Ltd.
P.O. Box 704, Windsor, NSW 2756, Australia

Printed in China

Sterling ISBN-13: 978-1-4027-4926-1
ISBN-10: 1-4027-4926-0

For information about custom editions, special sales,
premium and corporate purchases, please contact
Sterling Special Sales Department at 800-805-5489 or
specialsales@sterlingpublishing.com.

ii–iii: Don Hammond/Design Pics/Corbis, iv: Sandra
Seckinger/zefa/Corbis, 3: Roy Gumpel/Stone/Getty Image,
4: David Katzenstein/Corbis. 7: IPS Co., Ltd./Beateworks/
Corbis, 8–9: Mark Richards/ZUMA/Corbis, 11: Jupiter
Images, 12: A. Inden/zefa/Corbis, 14–15: Larry Williams/
zefa/Corbis, 16: DLILLC/Corbis, 18–19: Reichel Jean-Noel
Taxi/Getty Images, 20–21: Robert van der Hilst/Corbis,
23: Owen Franken/Corbis, 24: Gustavo Di Mario/Stone+/
Getty Images, 27: Theo Allofs/Corbis , 29: LWA-Dann
Tardif/Corbis , 31: Russell Underwood/Corbis, 32: Larry
Williams/zefa/Corbis, 34–35: Jupiter Images, 36: Jupiter
Images , 38–39: Emielke van Wyk/Gallo Images ROOTS
RF/Getty Images, 40–41: Joe McDonald/Corbis, 43: Bill
Denison/Solus-Veer/Corbis, 44: Cyril Ruoso/JH Editorial/
Minden Pictures/Getty Images, 47: Uli Wiesmeier/zefa/
Corbis, 48: Thorsten Milse/Robert Harding World
Imagery/Getty Images, 51: Melisa McKolay Photography,
52–53: David Edwards/National Geographic/Getty Images,
55: Image Source/Corbis, 56: Frans Lemmens/zefa/Corbis,
59: Kayoco/zefa/Corbis, 60: Karen Kasmauski/Corbis,
63: Matt Carr/Photonica/Getty Images, 64: Tom Brakefield/
Corbis, 66–67: Macduff Everton/Corbis, 68: Annie Griffiths
Belt/Corbis, 70–71: William Gottlieb/Corbis, 72v73: Ken
Redding/Corbis, 75: David Sacks/Stone/Getty Images,
76: Judy West , 78–79: Jupiter Images, 80: Don Hammond/
Design Pics/Corbis, 82–83: DLILLC/Corbis, 84: David
Hiser/Stone/Getty Images, 87: Altrendo Images/Altrendo/
Getty Images, 88–89: Christopher Arnesen/Stone/Getty
Images, 90–91: Hein van den Heuvel/zefa/Corbis

Cover and series design by woolypear